To DaD,

All ouh LovE

Ian, Angie,
RYan, Nicola

xx
x

Happy BiRtHDay

2oo5.

£3 00

Fighting Merchantman

BRITISH MERCHANT SHIPPING AT WAR
FROM WORLD WAR ONE TO THE FALKLANDS

SYDNEY GOODMAN

HALSGROVE

First published in Great Britain in 2001

British Library Cataloguing-in-Publication Data
A CIP record for this title is available from the British Library

ISBN 1 84114 1291

HALSGROVE
PUBLISHING, MEDIA AND DISTRIBUTION

Halsgrove House
Lower Moor Way
Tiverton, Devon EX16 6SS
Tel: 01884 243242
Fax: 01884 243325
email sales@halsgrove.com
website www.halsgrove.com

Printed in Great Britain by Bookcraft, Midsomer Norton

CONTENTS
SHIPS IN ALPHABETICAL ORDER

Acknowledgements

As with other publications of photographs from the Goodman Collection, this book does not cover every type of merchantman but is compiled from photographs selected from the collection that provide a wide chronological spread over a varied range of vessel types. It is intended to show pictures of ships that have served during wars and conflicts, and complements the earlier publications *Plymouth Warships* and *Portsmouth Warships*. *Fighting Merchantman* has come about because many former merchant navy men have requested that some of these types of ships be included in a book of their own. What is available in the collection has therefore been included in this book.

The author acknowledges the help of the administrators of the Goodman Collection, the Royal Navy PRO, the Royal Canadian Navy, *Warship International Fleet Review*, *Western Evening Herald*, Kevin Goodman, Devonport Naval Base Museum, and the P&O Steamship Company for their help in the preparation and research of this publication.

Foreword

If the phrase 'unsung heroes' is used to refer to any branch of Britain's fighting forces, it surely best applies to those who manned her merchant ships in times of war. While vast numbers of films, books, and television programmes have been dedicated to the courageous exploits of the regular forces, very little has been written about the part played by the ships and men who kept island Britain supplied with food and materials of war during the various conflicts of the last century. While individual convoys such as those bound for Russia and Malta have been accorded their place in history, the full story of the fighting merchantman is yet to be fully told.

The photographs included in this book are a reminder of just how reliant we are upon our merchant fleet in times of war. They show us too how every conceivable kind of vessel was called into action, many of which fell victim to enemy action. To this motley assortment of ships, and to the men who manned them, we as an island nation owe so much.

HMS LARGS

INTRODUCTION

The story of the merchant navy in war is a story of battles, not only with the enemy, but with the sea. Storms, ice, fog, enemy mines, torpedoes, aerial attacks and gunfire – all these had to be faced and overcome. The full story of the men and the ships who daily faced these dangers has, shamefully, never been told, and this book only goes some way towards paying the tribute to which they are due.

The merchant sailor went to sea at the age of 15. Many that began to learn their trade aboard troop-ships bound for the Boer War, and who served their country faithfully through the Great War of 1914–18, were still at sea during the Second World War. If he were asked if each war was more dangerous than the last he would surely answer 'yes', for developments in technical warfare brought new and greater threats to those whose trade was the sea. U-boats now worked in packs, torpedo bombers ranged miles out into the oceans – millions of tons of shipping were sunk in the early years between 1939–45, and thousands of lives lost in unimaginable circumstances.

Yet the crews of these ships, unglamorous compared to the Senior Service, underpaid and often unprotected, served under officers whose experience at sea in peacetime stood them in good stead throughout the years of conflict at sea. Taking the dangers and discomfort in their stride, their job was to shepherd their precious cargoes across miles of unforgiving sea, instill confidence in the men who served under them, and maintain discipline even in the most desperate of circumstances.

The merchant service is one which typically dislikes fuss, facing problems with equanimity and stoicism – but there is no typical merchant navy sailor. There are all sorts of master and many types of seaman, from the smart crew of a luxury liner to the coal-blackened 'salts' of a tramp steamer, each has its own code and superstitions of the sea. They come from the ports of the Mersey, the Clyde, South Wales, Hull, Glasgow, Plymouth, Falmouth, and the saying 'the sea is in his blood' is often true; seafaring is a trade, like many others, which runs in families.

When the war began many merchant ships were requisitioned by the Royal Navy to serve as armed merchant cruisers, or in other capacities. Fishing trawlers became minesweepers, pleasure craft were pressed into service as tenders and patrol craft. Many merchant officers and men were also drafted into the Royal Navy, men who had been either in the Royal Naval Reserve or were serving in vessels that became armed merchant cruisers – the ship changing its Red Ensign for the White.

War at sea is different from the conflict on land. At sea there are no lulls in the fighting, every hour of every day holds hidden and ever-present peril. The merchant marine suffered grievously, particularly in the Second World War, when the requirement to import food, oil, armaments, troops and equipment was essential in keeping Britain from the defeat suffered by the rest of Europe.

Merchant sailors also endured inequalities compared to other servicemen, and it seems incredible that they had their pay stopped the minute their ship was sunk. Even after spending days, even weeks, in lifeboats or on rafts, they were given nothing by way of compensation and those lucky enough to be rescued simply had to sign on for another trip, not knowing what type of ship they were to serve on until they saw her for the first time in port. Often ships were pressed into service that would otherwise have faced the scrapyard, although as the war progressed more and more new vessels were delivered from the shipyards of North America.

Whenever there is a conflict in which the Royal Navy becomes involved, there also will be the men and ships of the merchant navy to support them, combining their skills and resources under the three ensigns: Red, White and Blue. In wartime, before a convoy sailed, a conference was held with the Royal Navy. The Commodore of the Convoy looked down on the faces of the masters of the ships that were to sail under him. Some of them he knew from previous sailings, many were strangers. No one could say what dangers lay ahead but each master knew that observing the disciplines of sailing in convoy might mean the difference between life and death. Each also knew that the make-up of ships in the convoy would have a bearing on its success – the speed of the convoy being determined by the speed of the slowest ship.

Notices displayed around the walls of the conference room remind the officers of the practicalities of convoy life: 'Have you a blue bulb in your stern light?', 'Have you two white rockets ready to fire?' Despite the coming dangers the atmosphere in the room is relaxed. Among the masters are Americans, British, Norwegian, Swedish, Dutch and many other nationalities, each joined in a common purpose under the Allied command. One master states he is short of an engineer, another that he is effecting repairs to damage received during a run to Murmansk. Their attention is then drawn to the manner in which they should identify themselves when at sea, and to the lists of radio stations on friendly coasts. They then turn to their sailing orders, which instruct them that they must keep closed-up after passing through the boom to the open sea. Each master knows that any ship that lags behind is vulnerable to attack and incurs greater risk of being sunk. Radio silence is to be observed. Masters are instructed in the route to sail should they stray off course and become detached from the convoy, and are further provided with details of what escorts and air cover they will have. They are warned that good station-keeping is essential and, whilst stragglers will be nursed along, there will come a time when the safety of the convoy comes before that of individual ships. All this and a host of other information is given to the individual masters, but the responsibility for the safe passage of fifty or sixty ships lies in the hands of the Commodore.

The requisitioning of merchant ships, arming them with guns in home and foreign ports began immediately war was declared. Reservists and pensioners were mobilised, while merchant ship fabric was stiffened to take new guns. By the end of 1939 fifteen hundred guns had been mounted in a variety of merchant ships, and their gunners embarked. By the end of 1940 ships carrying anti-submarine guns exceeded four thousand.

Although the merchantman's chief task was to bring her cargo safely into port, the merchant navy had a long record of success against the enemy. U-boats had been sunk by gunfire and aircraft shot down into the sea. It was not only naval gunners that manned the guns, seamen themselves often took a gunnery course and over ten thousand merchant seamen became gunners, along with those that became merchant machine gunners. Not only were ships of the Red and Blue ensigns armed but also those of our allies, especially large liners that had been requisitioned as troop transports. These were usually more heavily armed than a tanker or a steamer.

The range of aircraft increased with the Liberator, Sunderland, Catalina and Hudson coming into service. The merchant seaman knew well the part played by aircraft and their crews and seeking out the U-boat menace. Armed with increasingly sophisticated weapons and air-to-surface radar the RAF began to score heavily against the German Navy. On approaching a convoy the first thing the aircraft would do was to identify itself to the convoy. The pilot would then fly up and down the lines of ships covering many square miles of sea counting their number. Often two or three different totals are arrived at so the pattern is repeated until the number is agreed upon. What a relief if none is missing! If a vessel was lost the Senior Naval Escort may signal to the aircraft with an Aldis lamp 'have you seen the other part of the convoy?' Or, 'will you go and look for our lame duck?' There is great relief when the straggler is brought back into the fold.

What the pilot hopes for is a sighting of a U-boat. Interminable searching of the seemingly empty sea, often out of sight of the convoy, sometimes led to the sighting of the wash from a submarine's bow, or the sinister shape of a U-boat beneath the surface. At this, the aircraft dives and makes ready to drop depth charges and, if the submarine dives, the aircraft calls up a nearby corvette which steams to the area to continue the attack.

Another duty of patrolling aircraft is searching and reporting survivors. Many merchant seamen have been grateful for the sight of a search plane that speeded their rescue. In the early stages of the war shipwrecked men often suffered the agonies of thirst, frostbite, starvation and exposure, with little hope of rescue. It was not unknown for the enemy to fire on survivors in open lifeboats and those in the water. Man's inhumanity to man reached unknown depths, but the tenacity of man fighting for his life has never more been clearly displayed by those who, once rescued, returned to crew new ships, often on more than one occasion.

A ship complete with men, machinery, cargo and stores is a complex mechanism. War further complicates her existence with the added dangers of the sea itself. New bunkering ports, cranage and docks, and navigation of unfamiliar waters brought new hazards. To meet these problems routing officers were needed to plan voyages and meet the resupply needs of the ship, be it cargo vessel, troopship, tanker or military tansport. It would not be unusual for a ship homeward bound from India to be redirected to Central America, there to load bauxite for North America, and in turn to reload a cargo for the United Kingdom.

Gradually new rules and orders came into force covering loading of cargoes in order to increase efficiency. The carrying of deck cargoes, the transport of cargo and passengers by troopship, all required vessels to undergo conversion or modification for their coming journeys. Certain deck cargoes had to be made weatherproof against the sea, ice and fire, and possible damage from enemy action. Such ships had also to be stable in all types of weather for it would be disastrous for a deck cargo of aircraft, trucks or tanks to break loose in rough seas. Many other problems had to be taken into consideration: the rolling of the ship in heavy weather, ballasting the ship correctly, the difference in summer and winter trim – a ship loaded with ore would sink like a stone if sea water entered her holds. Tankers often carried both a cargo of oil plus a deck cargo making a deadly combination should the ship be attacked.

All these factors, the control, routing and off-loading of ships, was part of the wartime introduction of vessels into the merchant navy. On arrival in port each ship was rescheduled for a named outward-bound convoy ready to meet all new problems, often on a voyage to unfamiliar waters that it had not been built to navigate. Peacetime passenger liners became armed merchant cruisers, troop carriers found themselves performing duties they were not designed for, with their interiors stripped out to increase the capacity of troops and equipment. Both RMS *Queen Elizabeth* and *Queen Mary* underwent the indignity of having their luxurious cabins stripped in order to accommodate more troops, while other passenger ships were fitted with gun platforms. Most merchant ships performed roles they were not designed for. RFAs carried fuel, water, armaments and food, along with spares for the fleet. Without their support many military operations and amphibious landings could not have taken place.

During both world wars the need was not only for deep-seagoing ships. Almost as vital were the coastal vessels, the cross-Channel ferries, trawlers, tugs, and many other types, perhaps less glamorous than their bigger sisters but just as important to the defence of our island. Indeed some of these were called upon to cross oceans, visiting waters they were never designed to sail. Cross-Channel ferries were converted to hospital ships, as were larger liners, while others became landing ships, minelayers, minesweepers, and fire floats. Fishermen and their trawlers were now catching a more deadly harvest, that of mines laid by enemy aircraft, submarines and other ships, their contribution to the war being just as vital as that of the troopship or tanker. Dunkirk remains the brightest example of what the

British seamen and their vessels could be called upon to achieve in time of need. Without them history might tell a different story.

As the sun sets, casting its pale light across the water, one by one ships move slowly out from their anchorage. From their funnels black columns of smoke begin to rise as tankers, tramps and munition ships form up into a convoy bound perhaps for Russia, the Mediterranean or the Far East. Soon they will be joined at sea by ships from other ports until the convoy is complete, while naval escort vessels begin their tasks of shepherding them. Submarine or air attack can come at any time, and there is the ever-present threat from the sea itself. Individual masters will not know of the disposition of enemy vessels but the Commodore will and all eyes will be on his vessel for signals by flag or Aldis lamp. Each ship will be on alert to alter course, to zigzag or otherwise, while also responding to orders from naval escorts telling the master to 'turn up the wick old man' if he is lagging behind, or standing by him in the event of engine trouble or failure. A master sailing in a convoy of many columns spread over many miles of sea can be ignorant of what happens on the far side of the convoy, and his only knowledge of attack may be the distant thud as a torpedo finds its target, or a tell-tale column of flame and smoke as another vessel is stricken.

Troopships were normally fast vessels that often sailed in convoys of ships of equal speed. But even these, at times, had to sail in convoy with slower ships, all steaming at the speed of the slowest ship in the convoy. All seamen realised that victory in war depended on the movement of supplies and equipment, and that without the convoys the war could not be won. Ships and their crews needed to be available at all times to meet these needs, not only from our own shores but also from America, Canada, India, Australia, New Zealand, South Africa and many other countries. The famous Malta convoys epitomised the courage and determination of all those who sailed on merchant vessels, keeping that vital island out of enemy hands.

The convoys to Russia by the northern route to Murmansk and Archangel also hold an honourable place in the history of this nation. Supplies that originated in America and Canada were shipped to the United Kingdom for forward passage to Russia. With Hitler demanding that these convoys be stopped at all cost, the crews of ships faced constant attacks from surface raiders, U-boats, torpedo bombers and bombers. But they also faced an equally implacable enemy in the arctic weather which so festooned the rigging with ice that ships were in danger of capsizing under its weight. To be sunk in the arctic meant almost certain death while many lost limbs through frostbite. By the end of 1941, 572 tanks, 800 fighter aircraft, 1410 vehicles and 100 000 tons of military cargo had been shipped to Russia. As time went by American, Polish, Dutch, Norwegian vessels, and ships of many other nations joined British and Russian ships. On the voyage to Archangel ice-breakers were necessary in the winter months, and seamen from warmer climes wore extra clothing even whilst carrying out their jobs as stokers.

Convoys bound for the Mediterranean ran the gauntlet from land-based aircraft and from submarines, although they did not have the arctic weather to contend with. These ships also had mines to add to their list of obstacles to overcome. Malta became an isolated outpost when Italy entered the war and Churchill identified the island as pivotal to Allied success in the war. Effectively if Malta was lost then the war was lost, and so every sacrifice was made to ensure the island received supplies. Vice Admiral James Somerville sent a message to each ship's master on one convoy that 'The convoy must go through'. Other orders included 'don't make smoke', 'don't show any lights at night', and 'if you have to send any signal by day or night use the lowest power light, keep good station and don't straggle.'

Victory in war depends on many factors including effective supply and rapid transport. The success of the Merchant Navy's undertaking is proved by the weight of men and metal brought across the oceans of the world, thus enabling Allied forces to defeat the enemy in the many theatres of war. As the troops moved eastward so did the support, the merchantman keeping pace with advances – ocean liners, tankers, tramps, colliers and coasters, fishing trawlers – all were needed. The total number of ships and craft of all kinds used in the landings in Sicily was 2700, many of these ships, especially coasters, spent years there before returning to home waters, much of their work being unspectacular but nonetheless vital.

Allied command of the sea around Europe, and in June 1944 during the invasion of Normandy, was crucial to the success of this great venture. Hundreds of merchant ships, including cross-Channel ferries fitted out as assault ships, coasters that had been strengthened, and tankers carrying bulk and cased petrol, stood off the French coast, together with ships of the Royal Navy and Allied navies. Some of the small vessels flying the Red Ensign had been among those that years earlier had brought our soldiers out of Dunkirk.

For the merchant navy the invasion of Europe signalled the culmination of its work, although the task was by no means completed. Throughout this time American forces and material was still being transported across the Atlantic by British, American and Allied ships, while around our coasts coal and other supplies were being delivered to ports for home and industrial use. Fishermen were still catching fish to supplement the nation's diet. The Merchant Navy had done all it could in supporting the armed forces and to this day in various ports around the world during any crisis the merchantman is ready to support the military.

A telling question remains: will this proud tradition continue as the number of ships under the Red Ensign diminishes? Recently, though, Government incentives have seen some companies registering vessels in the U.K.

RFA ABBEYDALE   Built by Swan Hunter, Wigham Richardson and completed in 1937, like many of her sisters during World War Two wherever the fleet went her support was called upon to transport and supply fuel.   November 1942 saw her supporting the North Africa landings – Operation Torch.   After the war had ended, the fleet was reduced in size and so was the the requirement for RFA support. Abbeydale was paid off and laid up until September 1960 when she arrived at T.W. Wards, Barrow, to be broken up.

HMS ALAUNIA   Built by John Brown, Clydebank, and launched in February 1925, she was requisitioned as an armed merchant cruiser in August 1939.   She was then fitted with eight 6-inch and two 3-inch guns, and served in this capacity until purchased by the Admiralty in February 1944.   She later underwent conversion to a repair ship, this being completed in September 1945.   She served until September 1957 when she arrived at Hughes Bolckow, Blyth, to be broken up.

RMS ALCANTARA Built by Harland and Wolff, Belfast, completed in 1936, she was requisitioned for service as an armed merchant cruiser on 25 September 1939 and fitted with eight 6-inch and two 3-inch guns.   On 28 July 1940 she and the German raider *Thor* fought an action during which both ships received damage. She was returned to trade on 29 June 1943, then in July 1943 she became a troopship for the Ministry of War Transport.

CS ALERT Built by Swan Hunter, Wigham Richardson, she was completed in 1918 for the GPO (Post Office). She was hired by the Admiralty in 1940 and came under their control. She was lost on 24 February 1945 in the North Sea, possibly by a torpedo from a U-boat or by fouling a mine.

MV ALYNBANK Built by Harland & Wolff, Govan, and launched in 1925 for the Bank Line, Andrew Weir & Company, she was requisitioned for naval service in October 1939 and underwent reconstruction for her new role. This was completed in August 1940 and after a period serving with the Irish Sea escort group she then joined the Home Fleet for service on the Russian convoy escort patrol. She later went to the Mediterranean for Operation Torch, returning to the United Kingdom in January 1943 for refit. On completion she returned to the Mediterranean and took part in the Salerno landings. Whilst homeward bound in October 1943 she shot down two German aircraft that had attacked the convoy she was escorting. On her arrival home she was reconverted to a merchantman. In May 1944 she was stripped out, and on 8 June 1944 she was the first ship sunk as a breakwater (Gooseberry 3, Gold Beach, Arromanches) during the Normandy landings. She was raised in December 1945 and towed to Troon where she was broken up.

SS AMBROSE Built in 1903 she was commissioned as an armed merchant cruiser on 10 December 1914. *Ambrose* was later purchased, on 20 October 1915, for conversion to a submarine depot ship, then becoming HMS *Ambrose*. On 1 June 1936 she was renamed *Cochrane* and became a base ship. She was sold in August 1946 and in November 1946 arrived at T.W. Ward's yard at Inverkeithing to be broken up.

RFA APPLELEAF Built by Workman Clarke and completed in November 1916, she was launched as the *Texol* but was renamed *Appleleaf* in 1917. She served until December 1947 when she was broken up.

SS ARGENTINA Built by Newport News in 1929 for the Mooremack South America Line, she served as a troopship and transport from January 1942 to March 1946 when she was returned to her owners.

HMT ARKWRIGHT Built in 1930 with a displacement of 370 tons she was one of the numerous fishing vessels that were requisitioned for service as minesweepers. She was fitted with a twelve-pounder gun on her bow plus other smaller armaments. She was requisitioned in August 1939 and served with the Royal Navy until December 1945 when she was sold for further service with the fishing fleet.

RMS AURANIA/HMS ARTIFEX Built by Swan Hunter, Wallsend and launched in February 1924 for the Cunard Steamship Company. She was requisitioned by the Admiralty on 30 August 1939 for service as an armed merchant cruiser and fitted with the same armament as her sister ship *Alaunia*. She was bought by the Admiralty in 1941 and then underwent conversion to a heavy repair ship and renamed *Artifex* in December 1942, she served with the Royal Navy as a repair ship until 1961 when she was sold and broken up in La Spezia, Italy.

ARY SCHEFFER/HMS ARY   Built in 1904 she was a coaster with a displacement of 642 tons. Requisitioned by the Admiralty in 1943 for service as a wreck dispersal vessel she was renamed *Ary*. She carried out these duties around the British coastline until handed to the Ministry of War Transport in April 1946 for disposal.

MV ATHLONE CASTLE   Built by Harland & Wolff, Belfast in 1936 for the Union Castle Steamship Company, she is pictured here after refit and return to her owners in 1946. She served throughout the Second World War as a troopship.

MV ATLANTIC CAUSEWAY/ATLANTIC CONVEYER These two vessels are included in order to highlight the book's title *Fighting Merchantman*. Seen here in 1982 the pictures show that, even in recent times, the Merchant Navy is called upon to support the Royal Navy when there is a need. Unfortunately *Atlantic Conveyer* was lost during the Falklands conflict along with her captain. *Atlantic Causeway* was returned to her owners after hostilities had ended and a new *Atlantic Conveyer* was built to replace the one lost.

RMS AUSONIA   Built by Armstrong Whitworth in 1921 for the Cunard Steamship Company, she was a sister ship of the *Aurania*. Requisitioned by the Admiralty in September 1939 for service as an armed merchant cruiser, she was later purchased by the Admiralty and from 27 March 1942 until April 1944 underwent conversion to a repair ship, serving in this capacity until paid off for disposal then sold and broken up in Spain in 1965. Above she is pictured as an armed merchant cruiser in 1940. The picture below is taken in the 1930s whilst a liner on the North American Service.

RFA BACCHUS(1) Built by Hamilton and launched in May 1915, she was a store carrier and served as such until May 1936 when she was renamed *Bacchus II*. Paid off from RFA service she was used as a bombing target until 15 November 1938 when she was sunk by the gunfire of HMS *Dunedin* off Alderney.

RFA BACCHUS(2) Built by Caledon Shipbuilders and launched 15 July 1936, she served throughout the war years in the many theatres of war, she continued her service after hostilities had ended until 1962 when she was sold commercially and renamed *Pulau Bali*.

HMS BEAULY FIRTH built by Redhead and launched on 24 August 1944, she was completed as a maintenance ship for the Royal Navy. Her service career was short. She was sold in 1948 and renamed *Stanfirth*.

RFA BEECHLEAF Built by Richardson and launched in October 1916 she served throughout the First World War. After the war, *Beechleaf*, along with many other naval and merchant ships, was laid up. She was sold to commercial interests in 1919.

RFA BELGOL Built by Irvine DD, Hartlepool, and launched on 23 April 1917. An early oiler she was to serve throughout the Second World War during which time this photograph was taken. Sold in June 1958 she arrived at Charlestown to be broken up.

HMT BEN EARN A 235 ton trawler built in 1916, she was requisitioned for service in the Second World War in February 1940. She served as a minesweeper until returned to her normal role as a fishing vessel in February 1946.

RFA BISHOPDALE Built by Lithgow and launched in March 1937 she was to serve throughout the Second World War. At the end of that conflict, and with the fleet much reduced in size, many RFAS were laid up pending disposal, but *Bishopdale* held on until January 1970 when she was sold.

RFA BOARDALE Built by Harland & Wolff, Govan, she was launched on 22 April 1937. She was to have a short life for on 30 April 1940 she grounded near Narvik and sank.

RFAS BRAMBLELEAF AND CHERRYLEAF Seen here at Malta in 1934, *Brambleleaf* was formerly the *Rumol* but was renamed in 1917. She was built by Lithgow and launched on 28 December 1916. Torpedoed and beached in June 1942 near Port Said, she was broken up at La Spezia in April 1953. *Cherryleaf* was formerly the *Persol* built by Raylton Dixon and launched in November 1916. Renamed in 1917, she served until 1947 when she was sold and again renamed, *Alan Clore*.

RFA BRITISH STAR Built by Swan Hunter and completed in 1917, in the earlier photograph she is pictured dazzle-painted during the First World War. In 1937 she was renamed *Olynthus* and served on many stations throughout the world during the Second World War. Surviving the war unscathed, she was sold in June 1946.

MV BRITISH DART AND BRITISH WYE Both ships were taken up from trade (STUFT ships – ships taken up from trade) during the Falklands conflict, both returned to their owners after the conflict ended.

RFA BROOMDALE Built by Harland & Wolff, Govan, and launched on 2 September 1937, she survived the Second World War and served until 1960 when she arrived in Belgium to be broken up.

RFA BROWN RANGER Built by Harland & Wolff, Govan, and launched on 12 December 1940 with a gross tonnage of only 3500 tons. Ships of this class served all over the world with the Royal Navy. She was sold for breaking up in 1975.

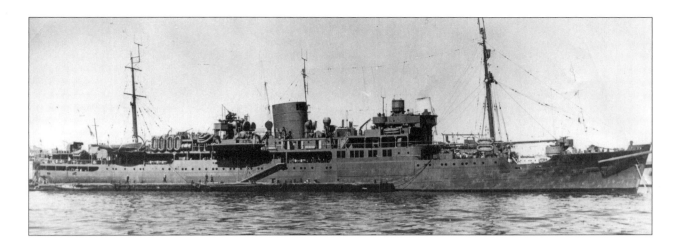

MV BULOLO Built by Curle in 1938 for Burns, Phillip & Co. she was requisitioned as an armed merchant cruiser on 22 September 1939. She also served as a Command Ship and on 25 March 1942 became a Headquarters Landing Ship. She was returned to her owners on 4 December 1946.

SS CALEDONIA Built by Alexander Stephens, Glasgow, for the Anchor Line (Henderson Brothers) and launched on 22 April 1923. She was requisitioned by the Admiralty on 30 August 1939 for service as an armed merchant cruiser and fitted with eight 6-inch and two 3-inch guns. She was also renamed *Scotstoun*. On 13 June 1940 she was attacked by U-25 and sunk in the Western Approaches.

SS CALIFORNIA Built by Alexander Stephens, Glasgow, for Anchor Line (Henderson Brothers) Ltd and launched on 17 April 1923. She was requisitioned on 25 August 1939 for service as an armed merchant cruiser and fitted with the same armament as the *Caledonia*. On 1 April 1942 she was returned to trade as a Ministry of War transport troopship. On 11 July 1943, whilst in convoy, she was bombed by German aircraft and set on fire, and next day, badly damaged, she was sunk by the escort destroyer HMS *Douglas*.

SS CANTON   Built by Alexander Stephens, Glasgow, for the Peninsular & Oriental Steam Navigation Co., she was launched on 14 April 1938.   Requisitioned on 19 October 1939 for service as an armed merchant cruiser, she was fitted with eight 6-inch and two 3-inch guns.   On 10 April 1944 she was returned to trade with the Ministry of War Transport as a troopship.   Returned to her owners on 28 September 1947 she continued to serve them until sold and broken up in Hong Kong in 1962.

RMS CAPETOWN CASTLE   Built by Harland & Wolff, Belfast for the Union Castle Mail Steamship Co. Ltd in 1938, she was requisitioned as a troopship.   At the end of the war she was refitted and returned to her owners to continue the mail service to South Africa.

RMS CARINTHIA Built by Vickers Ltd and completed in 1925 for Cunard White Star Line, *Carinthia* was requisitioned for service as an armed merchant cruiser in August 1939. On 6 June 1940 she was torpedoed by the U-46 south-east of Iceland and sank the following day.

RFA CEDARDALE Built by Blytheswood Shipbuilding, Glasgow, and launched 25 March 1939. Like so many ships of the RFA, wherever the Fleet was so also were they. She survived the Second World War and served until January 1960 when she arrived in Hong Kong to be broken up.

MV CHARLES PLUMIER (HMS LARGS) Built by Societe des Chantiers et Ateliers de Provence in 1938 for the French government, she was requisitioned in September 1939 for service as an armed merchant cruiser X-11, she was decommissioned on 22 November 1940. She was captured by HMS *Faulknor* off Gibraltar in late 1940 and handed to the Ministry of War Transport. She was renamed HMS *Largs* and fitted out as a landing ship. She was later returned to the French government and renamed *Charles Plumier* in 1948.

SS CHESHIRE Built by Fairfield and launched on 20 April 1927 for the Bibby Line. She was requisitioned on 29 August 1939 and fitted with six 6-inch and two 3-inch guns. She was returned to trade as a troopship on 9 June 1943 and in 1945 carried out the duties as a repatriation ship. She was returned to her owners on 5 October 1948.

SS CHITRAL Built by Alexander Stephens, Glasgow, for the Peninsular and Oriental Steam Navigation Co., and launched on 27 January 1925, she was requisitioned for service as an armed merchant cruiser on 30 August 1939. She was soon to see action, as on 20 November 1939 she intercepted the German *Bertha Fisser* south-west of Iceland which attempted to scuttle itself to avoid capture. *Chitral* shelled her and she drifted aground on fire on 21 November 1939. April 1944 saw her in use as a troopship. She was returned to her owners in 1948 and returned to commercial service until April 1953 when she arrived at Dalmuir to be broken up.

SS CILICIA   Built by Fairfield for the Anchor Line (Henderson Brothers), and launched on 21 October 1937.   *Cilicia* was requisitioned on 31 August 1939 and fitted with eight 6-inch and two 3-inch guns.   She was returned to trade as a troopship under the Ministry of War Transport on 16 February 1944, and in 1946 she was returned to her owners serving them until 1966 when she was sold to the Netherlands for service as a dockers' training ship and renamed *Jan Backx*, based in Rotterdam.   She was renamed *Cilicia* for her final journey to the breaker's yard in 1980 at Bilbao.

HMY CONQUEROR   A 900 ton yacht built in 1911, she was hired in September 1939 for service as an anti-submarine vessel and armed with one 4-inch, one 12-pounder and four 20-millimetre guns.   From 1941 to 1945 she served as an auxiliary anti-aircraft vessel.   She was returned to her owners in 1946.

SS CORINTHIAN Built by W. H. Gray & Co., West Hartlepool, and launched on 3 May 1938 for Ellerman & Papayanni Lines Ltd, she was hired for service as an ocean boarding vessel in September 1940 and fitted with two 6-inch, one 12-pounder, two 2-pounders and four 20-millimetre guns. She captured two enemy ships: in March 1941 the *Bijou Bihon* and in May 1941 the *Martin Pecheur*. She was then converted to a training ship and served as such until returned to her owners in 1945.

HMY CORSAIR Built in 1930 she was purchased by the Admiralty on 22 February 1940 for service with the FAA and served as an anti-submarine vessel in Bermuda. She was paid off in 1945 and placed on the sales list at Bermuda in December 1948.

LSS DAFFODIL Built by Armstrong Whitworth, Wallsend, and launched on 12 September 1917, she was formerly a train ferry. Purchased by the Admiralty in September 1940, both *Daffodil* and *Princess Iris* were used as LSSs (landing ship stern chute), and could carry 13 LCM(1)s (landing craft merchandised), or 9 LCM(3)s, and 105 troops. *Daffodil* was damaged by a mine off Dieppe on 17 March 1945 and sank the next day.

RFA DELPHINULA (ex BUYO MARU) An early tanker she was first listed by the RFA in 1921. In 1939 she was hulked and served as an oil hulk until 1947 when she was disposed of and broken up.

RFAS DEWDALE AND ENNERDALE Both vessels were converted in wartime to Landing Ship (Gantry). During construction, *Dewdale* at Cammell Laird and *Ennerdale* at Swan Hunter, each vessel was armed with one 4.7-inch, three 2-pounders and six 20-millimetre guns. They could carry fifteen LCM(1)s and 215 troops. Both survived the war. *Dewdale* was scrapped at Antwerp in December 1959 and *Ennerdale* at Faslane in April 1959.

RFA EASEDALE Built by Furness Shipbuilders and launched on 18 December 1941 she served throughout the war and early post-war years. Along with so many of her sister naval ships she was paid off then hulked until 1960 when she was sold for breaking up.

SS EL CIERVO Built by Sir W.G. Armstrong later Whitworth & Co. for the Lobitos Oilfields Ltd, and launched in 1923. *El Ciervo* is pictured here in dry dock under repair after being torpedoed, one of the principal dangers merchant ships and their crews faced whether in convoy or sailing alone. She later returned to service.

A selection of empire ships that served in many capacities, the prefix EMPIRE was carried by a multitude of ships from tugs to troopships. In this selection we have the *Empire Bure, Empire Helford, Empire Parkestone (p.47), Empire Pride, Empire Test, Empire Toiler (p.48)* and *Empire Wansbeck (p.49)*.

SS EMPIRE PROTECTOR Built by Furness Shipbuilding and launched on 20 July 1944, her name was changed to *Wave Protector* in 1945 when all the Empire Class were transferred to the Ministry of Transport then later to the Royal Fleet Auxiliary. In March 1958 she became an oil hulk serving in this capacity until 1953 when she was broken up in Italy.

RFA FRANCOL Built by Earles and completed in 1917. Whilst on active service in the Far East in 1942 she was attacked by Japanese aircraft then shelled by Japanese cruisers and destroyers and sank south of Java.

RFA FORTOL   Built by MacMillan & Sons, Dumbarton, and completed in 1917, *Fortol* served throughout the Second World War. She was broken up at Rosyth in 1958.

SS FOSSBECK   Built by Smith's Dock and launched 11 April 1930 for the Foss Beck Shipping Co. Ltd. She was hired by the Admiralty in November 1939 as an aircraft transport but in 1942 she became a boom carrier. She was returned to her owners in 1946.

HMT GOLDEN MILLER A steam drifter built in 1910, she was hired by the Admiralty in November 1939 to serve as an armed patrol drifter. *Golden Miller* served in this capacity until September 1945 when she was returned to her owners.

PS GLEN AVON Built in 1912 she was to serve in two world wars. From 4 November 1914 to 5 July 1919 *Glen Avon* served as a minesweeper and was hired again in September 1939 for service as an anti-aircraft ship and also carried out anti-submarine patrols and minesweeping duties. She was fitted with numerous armaments for this role including depth charges. She foundered in a gale on 2 September 1944 off the Seine estuary.

SS GLENEARN, GLENROY AND GLENGYLE All three ships were built for the Glen Line Ltd in 1938, the *Glenearn* and *Glengyle* by Caledon Shipbuilders, and the *Glenroy* by Scotts Shipbuilding & Engineering. All three were hired by the Admiralty in 1939 as fast transports but were to serve as assault ships, LSI(L)s or command ships. They were to take part in many operations including transporting the BEF to France and Greece, and on supply runs to Malta, They also took part in the ill-fated Dieppe raid. *Glenearn* and *Glenroy* both sustained damage during the war but all were returned to their owners in 1946.

RFA GOLD RANGER Built by Caledon Shipbuilding and launched on 12 March 1941, of 3300 tons this class was to serve on many foreign and home stations. She survived the war and served until sold in March 1973.

RFA GREEN RANGER Built by Caledon and launched in August 1941, she survived the war but in November 1962, whilst being towed to a Welsh shipyard for refit, she was wrecked near Hartland Point and broke in two as the second picture shows.

SY HELIOPOLIS   Built in 1903, she was purchased by the Admiralty on 23 February 1940 for use as a Fleet Air Arm target. She served until 1946 when she was placed on the disposal list and sold.

MV HELVIG   Built by Helsingörs Jernskibs-og, Denmark, and completed in 1937, she was seized in May 1940 and fitted out as a motor launch depot ship.   In April 1941 she became a seaward defence vessel until she was returned to her owners in April 1946.

RFA HICKEROL Built by MacMillan, Dumbarton and launched on 30 November 1917, *Hickerol* was one of the fuel tankers that provided the Royal Navy with a coastal supply service. She lasted until 1948 when sold commercially and renamed *Hemsley II*.

MV HIGHLAND CHIEFTAIN Built by Harland & Wolff, Belfast, and launched in 1929 for the Royal Mail Lines. One of five sisters that were to serve as troopships during the Second World War, *Highland Patriot* was a war loss whilst *Highland Brigade*, *Chieftain*, *Monarch* and *Princess* were all returned to their owners in 1946 for further service.

SS HILARY Built by Cammell Laird and launched in 1931 for the Booth Steamship Co. Ltd, *Hilary* was requisitioned as an ocean boarding vessel until April 1942 during which time she intercepted or captured several enemy ships. She was then refitted as a landing ship, serving as such until March 1946 when she was returned to her owners.

SS ISLE OF JERSEY A cross-Channel packet requisitioned for use as a hospital ship. Many such vessels and their crews went quietly about their duties often in hazardous circumstances. Most never had a mention but they were there for the injured when needed.

HMT JACINTA   Another veteran trawler that saw service in two world wars. She was hired for service as an armed patrol vessel from 1915 to 1919 and again hired in May 1940, then purchased. *Jacinta* served as a minesweeper until January after which she became a wreck dispersal vessel. She was sold in May 1946.

SS KARANJA Built by Alexander Stephens, Glasgow, and launched in 1931 for the British India Steam Navigation Co. She was requisitioned by the Admiralty in 1940 as a troopship then in July 1941 she was converted to an LSI (Landing Ship Infantry). 1942 was to prove a busy but fatal year for her as she took part in the capture of Diego Saurez and later in Operation Torch. On 12 November 1942, whilst off Bougie, she was bombed by German aircraft and sunk.

SS KENYA/HMS KEREN Built by Stepan and launched on 27 August 1930, she was hired by the Admiralty and renamed *Hydra*. In July 1941 she was converted to a landing ship (LSI), and in October 1941 she was renamed *Keren*. She took part in many operations including Operation Torch and the Allied landings in southern France. In April 1946 *Keren* was purchased by the Admiralty and then taken over by the Ministry of War Transport. She was sold in 1946.

HMT KINDRED STAR A drifter built in 1930, she was hired by the Admiralty for service as a minesweeper in December 1939, serving as such until 1946 when she was returned to her owners.

RFA KIMMEROL Built by Craig Taylor, Stockton-on-Tees, and launched 4 April 1916, she was one of the many smaller oilers in RFA service. *Kimmerol* displaced 2400 tons and served until 1949 when she was sold and renamed *Tenana*.

RFA KURUMBA Built by Swan Hunter and launched on 14 September 1916. As oil-fired ships became more numerous in the Royal Navy so oilers were needed to transport and distribute fuel to meet the needs of the Fleet. She saw service with the Royal Australian Navy. She served until 1948 when she was sold.

HMT KUROKI Built in 1909 she was another trawler that was to see service in the two world wars. She was hired in 1915, serving until 1919. Hired again in January 1940 she saw service as a boom defence vessel, remaining in this role until July 1945 after which she was returned to her owners.

SS LANCASHIRE Built by Harland & Wolff, Belfast, and launched in 1917 as a troopship for the Bibby Brothers, she continued with these duties until requisitioned at the start of the Second World War. *Lancashire* served as an accommodation ship until paid off for disposal after the war had ended.

HMT LORD INCHCAPE Built in 1924 she was hired by the Admiralty in August 1939 for service as a minesweeper. On 25 October 1940 she was sunk by a mine off Plymouth. She was later raised and purchased by the Admiralty and continued to serve until sold in August 1946.

LIBERTY SHIP A Liberty ship arrives in a North African port and LCTs are busy unloading the stores etc. she has brought in order to give her a quick turn-around as she may be needed for another convoy, or involved in another landing in the Mediterranean or Middle East.

SS LLANDOVERY CASTLE   Built by Barclay Curle & Co. Glasgow in 1925 for the Union Castle Mail Steamship Company.   She was requisitioned by the Admiralty in 1940 and converted to hospital ship No. 39.   She was returned to her owners in September 1946 and continued to serve them until 1953 when sold for breaking up.

MERCHANTMAN SINKING An unknown merchantman has been torpedoed and is listing heavily to starboard. The crew can be seen making their way down the portside.

SS PANAMA/HS MAINE Built by Fairfields and launched in 1902 she was purchased by the Admiralty in 1920. In 1921 she underwent conversion to a hospital ship and was manned by the RFA. She served in this capacity until paid off and was sold for demolition, arriving at McClellands, Bowness, on 8 July 1948 to be broken up.

SS MALOJA Built by Harland & Wolff, Belfast, and launched on 19 April 1923 for the Peninsular & Oriental Steam Navigation Company. She was hired by the Admiralty on 11 September 1939 for service as an armed merchant cruiser, being fitted with eight 6-inch and two 3-inch guns. On 13 March 1940 she intercepted the *La Coruna* which had been set on fire to avoid capture, she was then shelled by *Maloja* and sunk. In November 1941 she was returned to the Ministry of War Transport and fitted out as a troopship. After the war she was returned to her owners for further service which lasted until April 1954 when she was sold and broken up at Faslane.

MV MANUNDA Built by Beardmore and completed in 1930 for the Adelaide Steamship Company of Australia. She was requisitioned for service as a hospital ship in May 1940. In February 1942 whilst at Darwin, her hospital ship markings clearly visible, she was bombed by Japanese aircraft and damaged. She was returned to her owners in September 1946 and continued trading until 1956 whe she was sold for further service and renamed *Hokan Maru*. She never traded under this new name and was sold and broken up in Japan in 1957.

HMT MARIA Built in 1929 she was formerly the German August Wriedt, she was captured on 29 May 1941, in March 1942 she was commissioned into RN service as a wreck dispersal vessel. She was broken up in June 1951.

SS MAUNGANUI Built by Fairfields in 1911 for the Union Steamship Company of New Zealand. Serving as a hospital ship, not strictly a fighting merchantman, she nonetheless qualifies as a merchantman requisitioned for wartime service. She served in this capacity from 1941 until August 1946 after which she was laid up at Wellington. *Maunganui* was later sold for further service as the Panamanian flagged *Cyrenia*.

RMS MAURETANIA Built by Cammell Laird and launched in 1938 for the Cunard Steamship Company, she was requisitioned by the Admiralty and sent to Sydney, Australia, for conversion to a troopship. She served as such until released by the Ministry of War Transport, was then refitted and returned to her owners. Her first post-war crossing to New York from Liverpool was on 26 April 1947. She was sold in 1965 and arrived at T.W. Ward's yard at Inverkeithing on 23 November 1965 to be broken up.

SS MENESTHEUS   Built by Caledon Shipbuilding, Dundee, and launched in 1929 for the Ocean Steamship Co. Ltd, she was requisitioned by the Admiralty on 14 December 1939 and fitted out as a minelayer.   She carried two 4-inch, twelve 20-millimetre guns and 410 mines.   *Menestheus* served in this role until late 1944 when she was refitted for a new role as an amenities ship for Pacific operations.   Operating from forward bases that had no normal shore facilities, she provided recreational facilities superior to that of a normal depot ship.   During this period of service from February 1945 until July 1946 she flew the Red Ensign.   She was returned to her owners in August 1946.

HMT MILFORD QUEEN Built in 1917 she was formerly the RN *William Browis*. Requisitioned in 1939 for minesweeping duties she was returned to her owners in December 1945.

RFAs MIXOL AND THERMOL *Mixol* was built by Greenock and Grangemouth Company and was launched on 17 June 1916. One of the workhorses of the RFA fleet, she survived the Second World War and was sold in 1947 and renamed *White Rock*. *Thermol* was built by Caledon Shipbuilding, Greenock, and launched on 29 April 1916. A sister to *Mixol,* she served until 1946 when she was taken over by the Ministry of Transport.

SS MONTCALM Built by John Brown and launched on 3 July 1920 for the Canadian Pacific Railway Company, she was requisitioned by the Admiralty on 17 October 1939. In 1942 she underwent conversion to a submarine depot ship, then was purchased by the Admiralty and renamed *Wolfe*. She served with the 3rd Submarine Flotilla until 1944 when she joined the Eastern Fleet. Paid off for disposal she arrived at Faslane in November 1952 to be broken up.

SS MORETON BAY Built by Vickers Ltd and launched 23 April 1921 for the Australian Commonwealth Line. In 1928 she was sold to the White Star Line then in 1933 transferred to the Aberdeen and Commonwealth Line. She was requisitioned by the Admiralty in 1939 as an armed merchant cruiser and fitted with seven 6-inch and two 3-inch guns. On 20 August 1941 she was converted to a troopship and took part in many North African and European operations. She was returned to her owners in 1946 for further service and was broken up at Barrow in 1958.

HMT MOY Built by Cochranes and launched 22 May 1917 as the *Alexander Hills,* a 'Mersey' type trawler. She was renamed Moy in 1920. During the Second World War she was used as a minesweeper. She was sold in November 1946 and renamed *Coral Island*.

HMT NORTHCOATES Built by Cox and launched in 1918 as the *George Corton*, a 'Castle' type trawler, she was sold in 1921 and renamed *Zencon*. Hired by the Admiralty in 1939 for minesweeping duties, on 2 December 1944 she was damaged and foundered in tow.

HMS NAIRANA Laid down as a short sea passenger vessel she was completed by Denny in 1916 and purchased by the Admiralty as a seaplane carrier. She saw action in the North Sea and White Sea, she was sold in 1920 and converted to a passenger ship for the Tasmanian Steamship Co.

SS NIEUW AMSTERDAM Built by Rotterdam DD and launched in 1938 for the Nederlandsch-Amerikaansche Stoomvaart Maatschappij (Holland Amerika Lijn), she became an allied troopship in 1940 under Cunard management. She was returned to her owners in 1946 and continued commercial sailings.

MV NORLAND One of the North Sea ferries or STUFT ship (ship taken up from trade) that went to the Falkland Islands during the conflict in 1982. During her service there she was at the San Carlos landings and also made voyages to Uruguay, Argentina and Ascension Island. She returned to her owners in February 1983 to continue her North Sea sailings.

RFA OLNA(1) Built at Devonport Dockyard under the Colwyn Committee's recommendation that surplus facilities in Royal Dockyards be used to build merchant ships. She was completed in October 1921. On 18 May 1941 she was bombed by German aircraft and set on fire in Suda Bay where she was beached and burnt out. On 31 May 1941 she was seized by the Germans. In May 1945 the wreck was broken up at Skaramanga.

RFA OLNA(2) Built by Swan Hunter and launched 28 December 1944. After the war had ended she continued to serve the fleet until new constructions had been built, but the writing was on the wall as heavy fleet fuel oil was being reduced as newly built warships were using new modes of propulsion.

SS ONTRANTO Built by Vickers Armstrong, Barrow-in-Furness, for the Orient Line in December 1925. She was requisitioned by the Admiralty in 1939 for trooping, and 1942 saw her undergo conversion to an assault ship. She was present at the landings in North Africa, at Sicily and Salerno. After the war she continued trooping duties until returning to her owners where she was used on the Australian emigrant service. She paid off for disposal and arrived at Faslane to be broken up in 1957.

SS ORION Built by Vickers Armstrong Ltd, Barrow-in-Furness, for the Orient Steam Navigation Co. Ltd. In September 1939 she was taken over to serve as a troopship. She was returned to her owners in 1946. On 2 May 1960 Orient Lines merged with the Peninsular & Oriental Steam Navigation Company, today referred to as P&O. She was sold in 1963 and after a brief spell as an hotel ship at Hamburg she was broken up in Belgium.

HMT OYSTERMOUTH CASTLE   Completed in 1914 as a trawler she served in both world wars. In the 1939-45 conflict she was first used as an armed boarding vessel until converted to a minesweeper. She remained in this service until January 1946 when she was returned to her owners.

MV PALOMARES Built by Doxfords for MacAndrews & Co. Ltd in 1938, she was requisitioned in August 1940 and fitted out as an anti-aircraft ship. Late in 1942 she was refitted and emerged as an aircraft direction ship, serving until April 1946 when she was returned to her owners.

RFA PEARLEAF Built by W. Gray & Sons as the *Gypol* but renamed in 1917. Her outline is not one that ship lovers of today would recognise as a tanker, though she was an Admiralty oiler. She survived the Second World War and arrived at the breaker's yard of Hughes Bolckow at Blyth on 23 December 1947 to be broken up.

RFA PERTHSIRE Built in 1893 she was purchased by the Admiralty on 28 October 1914 and was then disguised as a dummy battleship. In 1915 she was refitted as a water carrier under RFA control, then became an oiler, and later in 1921 a store carrier. She was sold and broken up in Italy in 1934.

RFA PHILOL Built by Tyne Iron Shipbuilding Company and launched on 5 April 1916, she served as an oiler until 1956 when she was reduced to an oil hulk, remaining as such until sold in 1967 to be broken up.

RFA PLUMLEAF Built by Swan Hunter, Wigham Richardson in 1917 as the *Trinol* later being renamed in 1917. During the Second World War she was bombed whilst at Malta on 4 April 1942, during an Italian air attack. She sank to deck level and was then used as an oil jetty until raised in November 1946 and broken up.

MV POZARICA Built by Doxford in 1938, she was requisitioned for service as an anti-aircraft ship in June 1940, her conversion taking until March 1941. During her working-up period she collided with the Canadian destroyer *Restigouche* and after repairs joined the Western Approaches Command. In May 1942 she again collided, this time with a merchant ship and was taken to Belfast for repairs. On completion she joined the Russian Convoy PQ17 during which she came under attack from aircraft, shooting one down herself but suffering bomb damage. She again underwent refit and later took part in Operation Torch and then worked escorting convoys. On 29 January 1943 she was attacked by torpedo bombers and badly damaged. She was towed to Bougie on 1 February 1943 and beached, and a week or so later capsized. In February 1949 salvage operations began. She was raised on 5 March 1951, and on 14 June 1951 arrived at Savona to be broken up.

RFA PRESTOL   Built by Napier & Miller and launched on 4 September 1917, oilers of this type transported fuel oil to and from oil-producing countries as well as to naval bases around the world. She survived the Second World War and was sold in 1958, arriving at White's, St Davids, to be broken up.

MV PRETORIA CASTLE   Built by Harland & Wolff, Belfast, for the Union Castle Mail Steamship Company Ltd, and launched on 12 October 1938. She was requisitioned by the Admiralty on 2 October 1939 for service as an armed merchant cruiser. On 18 June 1940 she captured the French steamer *Desirade* off St Helena, and on 15 August 1941, in company with HMS *Despatch*, intercepted the German steamship *Norderney* in the Amazon estuary, the latter scuttling itself to avoid capture. She was paid off in August 1942 and converted to an escort carrier after purchase by the Royal Navy. Following the war she was sold to her original owners and after refit was renamed *Warwick Castle* and resumed normal sailings to South Africa.

SS PRINCE BAUDOUIN Built in 1934 she was in service as a Belgian cross-Channel ferry before being hired in 1940 to serve as an air target until July 1941. Later she was refitted as a landing ship infantry (LSI) serving in this capacity until returned to her owners in October 1945. She was present at the landings in southern France (Operation Torch) and the Normandy landings.

SS PRINCESSA Built by Alexander Stephens, Glasgow, in 1918 for the Furness-Houlder Argentine Lines Ltd, she survived the war and is pictured here being towed up the Bristol Channel in October 1946. She had boiler trouble but also there had been an alleged mutiny on board and police were waiting for her when she docked.

SS PRINCE CHARLES Built in 1930 she was hired as a landing ship infantry (LSI) in September 1940, serving until December 1944. She took part in operations from Norway to Normandy. After the war she was returned to her owners.

SS PRINCE DAVID Built by Cammell Laird in 1930 for Canadian National Steamships Ltd, she was hired as an armed merchant cruiser (RCN) in November 1939. In January 1940 she was purchased by the Royal Canadian Navy and was later converted to a landing ship infantry (M). She was placed on the sales list in January 1946 and sold, being renamed *Charlton Monarch* in 1948.

SS PRINCE LEOPALD Built by Cockerill in 1929 and serving as a Belgian cross-Channel packet, she was hired in 1940 as an air target. She was converted to a landing ship infantry (S) in 1941, and took part in the Salerno landings, attacks on Norway, the raid on Dieppe, the landings in Sicily and the Normandy landings. She was sunk by a U-boat in the English Channel on 29 July 1944.

SS PRINCE ROBERT Built by Cammell Laird in 1930 for the Canadian National Steamships Company Ltd, she was taken over for service as an armed merchant cruiser (RCN) in October 1939. Later purchased by the Canadian Royal Navy, in 1943 she was converted to an anti-aircraft ship. She was sold in October 1946 and renamed *Charlton Sovereign*.

SS PRINSES BEATRIX Dutch built in 1939 and hired by the Admiralty as a landing ship infantry (LSI) in August 1940, she served as such until April 1946 when returned to her owners. She was present at many landings including the Lofoten Islands, North Africa and Anzio.

SS PRINSES JOSEPHINE CHARLOTTE Built in 1931 for the Belgian cross-Channel service, she was hired as a landing ship infantry (S) in 1940. She was fitted with eight LCAs and could carry 250 troops. She was to take part in many operations, eventually returning to her owners in 1945.

QUEEN OF BERMUDA Built by Vickers Armstrong, Newcastle, for Furness Withy & Co. Ltd and launched 1 September 1932. She was requisitioned by the Admiralty on 30 August 1939 for service as an armed merchant cruiser, serving in this capacity until May 1943 when she was returned to the Ministry of War Transport who then employed her on troopship duties. During her period as an AMC she was based on the South Atlantic Station where part of her duties was to protect the whaling fleet and shore installations. One period saw her escorting the whalers to Freetown then to the United Kingdom, this patrol taking five months without relief. She was handed back to her owners in 1945. When built she had three funnels, but lost one of these during her naval service.

RMS QUEEN MARY Built by John Brown and launched on 26 September 1934 for the Cunard White Star Line. At the outbreak of the Second World War she was requisitioned as a troopship which was to take her to parts of the world her designers had not envisaged, including the Far East, Australia etc.

She and her sister *Queen Elizabeth* carried over one-and-a-quarter-million servicemen and women to and from the various theatres of war. The only incident in her wartime service was the collision with HMS *Curacao*. After the war she was refitted and returned to her owners to continue her transatlantic service. By the late 1960s airliners had made inroads to this traffic and she left Southampton on 31 October 1967, bound for Long Beach, California, to take up her new role as an hotel and convention centre. She is still in use today drawing many thousands of visitors every year. (p.101-102)

RMS QUEEN ELIZABETH Built by John Brown and launched on 27 September 1938 for the Cunard White Star Line, she was due to make her maiden voyage to New York on 24 April 1940. The war intervened and she left her builders without any trials, setting off across the Atlantic for New York to meet up with her sister. She was requisitioned as a troopship and after the war was refitted and returned to her owners. Her first Atlantic crossing began on 16 October 1946 and she continued until 1968 when she left Southampton for the last time bound for Port Everglades, Florida. Here she remained for several years before being bought by the C.Y. Shipping Group of Hong Kong. During conversion to a floating university in Hong Kong she caught fire and became a total loss. She was broken up where she lay in the harbour. (p.103-104)

RMS QUEEN ELIZABETH 2 Even in this age of modern warfare passenger ships are sometimes called upon to transport troops to wherever a conflict may be. The QE2 was adapted to carry helicopters when she was pressed into service during the Falklands crisis. The picture shows she had been fitted with helicopter landing platforms.

PS QUEEN EMPRESS Built in 1912 she was another veteran that saw service in two world wars. During the First World War she was hired as a minesweeper, serving from 25 October 1915 until returned to her owners on 30 June 1920. She was also hired on 27 October 1939, again for minesweeping duties, and in 1942 became an anti-aircraft ship. She was laid up in May 1944 and returned to her owners in May 1945.

HMY RADIANT A private yacht built in 1927, she was hired in September 1939 for anti-submarine duties. She then underwent a short refit before becoming a radar training ship, serving as such until June 1945.

MV RANGATIRA   One of the many STUFT ships (ship taken up from trade) during the Falklands conflict for ferrying troops and equipment to the South Atlantic. She was returned to her owners at the end of hostilities.

MV RANGITIKI Built by John Brown and launched in 1929 for the New Zealand Shipping Co. Ltd, she was requisitioned in December 1940 for service as a troopship. April 1945 saw her employed on repatriation and trooping duties. She was returned to her owners in 1947, taking up her commercial service in 1948. During her time as a troopship she was one of the ships in the convoy in which the *Jervis Bay* engaged the *Admiral Scheer*. *Rangitiki* escaped. She was broken up at Santander in 1962.

RFA RAPIDOL Built by Grays and launched on 23 April 1917, she served the Fleet pre-war and post-war until 13 March 1948 when she was sold for further trading and renamed *Louise Moller*.

Mrs Reeve cuts the ribbon at the naming of Ranpura Building watched by Commodore Reeve (far left), Captain Jon Harries CFM and members of the SWAT team.

SS RANPURA Built by R & W Hawthorn Leslie, Hebburn, and launched on 13 September 1924 for the Peninsular & Oriental Steam Navigation Company, she was requisitioned for Admiralty service as an armed merchant cruiser on 5 September 1939. She was then purchased and later converted to a fleet repair ship, serving in this capacity until she arrived at Spezia on 25 May 1961 to be broken up. (p.111-112)

SS RAWALPINDI Built by Harland & Wolff, Govan, and launched on 26 March 1925 for the Peninsular & Oriental Steam Navigation Co. She was requisitioned by the Admiralty on 26 August 1939 for service as an armed merchant cruiser. On 23 November 1939, whilst escorting a convoy south-east of Iceland she was attacked by the German pocket battleships *Scharnhorst* and *Gneisenau*. She fought them bravely allowing her convoy to scatter to avoid being sunk.

MV REINA DEL PACIFICO Built by Harland & Wolff, Belfast, and launched in 1931 for the Pacific Steam Navigation Company Ltd. She was requisitioned by the Admiralty for use as a troopship, carrying out this service until 1945. During 1946 she became a repatriation ship until 1947 when she was returned to her owners.

RFA RELIANT Formerly the *London Importer,* she was purchased for use as a store carrier by the Admiralty on 24 March 1933. Her wartime service saw her in many theatres of operations. In April 1948 she was sold and renamed *Anthony 6.*

RFA RESURGENT Formerly the MV *Chungchow*. In post-war years there have been many conflicts around the world and wherever the Fleet went she and her sister, *Retainer* (ex-*Chungking*) were there to perform their duties. She was scrapped in March 1981. Her sister was broken up in October 1979.

RFA ROBERT DUNDAS Built by Grangemouth Dockyard and launched on 28 July 1939, throughout her service life she delivered stores etc. to various home ports and other naval bases. She was paid off in 1972 and arrived at Grays, Essex to be broken up in July 1972.

MV ROYAL DAFFODIL Built by Denny, Dumbarton, and launched in 1934. She was hired by the Admiralty and took part in the evacuation of the British Expeditionary Force from Dunkirk in May 1940.

HMS ROYAL EAGLE Built by Cammell Laird and launched on 24 February 1932, she was hired by the Admiralty as an accommodation ship on 23 October 1939. In February 1940 she became an anti-aircraft vessel, also serving in other capacities, until May 1945 when she was returned to her owners (as *PS Royal Eagle*).

MV ROYAL SCOTSMAN Built by Harland & Wolff and launched on 11 March 1936, she was hired by the Admiralty as a store carrier in October 1940 and later fitted for use as a landing ship infantry (H) and could carry six LCAs and 830 troops. She was present during Operation Torch, the landings in North Africa, and the landings in Sicily and Salerno. She was returned to her owners in May 1945.

RFA RUTHENIA Built in 1900 as the *Lake Champlain*, she was purchased by the Royal Navy on 1 November 1914 to serve as the dummy battleship *King George V*. She was then converted to a water carrier in 1915 and an oiler in 1920. From 26 March 1931 she became an oil hulk at Singapore. On the fall of the island she was captured by the Japanese and renamed *Choran Maru*. She was recovered in 1946 and broken up in June 1949.

SAINFOIN/EMPIRE CROSSBOW Built by C.S.C. Wilmington and launched on 30 November 1943 as the *Cape Washington*, she was renamed *Sainfoin* in November 1944 on conversion to use as a landing ship. After the war had ended she was returned to the United States Navy.

SS SAMARIA Built by Cammell Laird & Co. and launched in 1921 for the Cunard Steamship Company, she was requisitioned by the Admiralty for service as a troopship from 1940 to 1948. *Samaria* was also used on government service for repatriation purposes. She was returned to her owners in 1948 and continued on Cunard passenger services until sold in 1956 to be broken up at Inverkeithing.

RFA SCOTOL Built by the Tyne Iron Shipbuilding Company and launched on 23 June 1916, she served the Fleet Auxiliary until November 1947 when she was sold and renamed *Hemsley I*.

MY SHEMARA Built in 1938 she was requisitioned by the Admiralty in September 1939 for use as an anti-submarine yacht. She was then used, from 1941 to March 1946, for anti-submarine training. Following the war she was returned to her owners.

RFA SIR GALAHAD Pictured here leaving Plymouth bound for the Falkland Islands in 1982 during which conflict she was attacked and lost with tragic loss of life amongst the crewmen and soldiers on board.

RFA SLAVOL Built by the Greenock & Grangemouth Company and launched on 21 April 1917 for service as a water carrier. In 1942 she was attacked and sunk by U205 north-east of Sullom Voe, Scotland. The lower photograph shows her anchored off Mauritius before the Second World War.

MV SOBIESKI Built by Swan Hunter, Wigham Richardson, Wallsend and launched in 1939, the following September she was hired by the Admiralty for service as a troopship. She was later fitted out as a landing ship infantry (L). After the war she underwent refit and was returned to her owners the Gydnia-America Shipping Lines, Poland, in 1947.

MV SPRINGBANK Built by Harland & Wolff, Govan, and launched on 13 April 1926 for the Bank Line, Andrew Weir & Company. She was requisitioned for Admiralty service in November 1939 and was fitted with armaments and a catapult for a Fairey Fulmar aircraft. While escorting convoy HG73 in the North Atlantic on 27 September 1941 she was attacked by German Kondor aircraft and then by the U201 which torpedoed her. Badly damaged she had to be sunk by the escorting corvette HMS *Jasmine*.

SS ST HELIER Built by Clydebank and launched on 26 March 1925, she was hired by the Admiralty as a landing ship infantry (H) in 1941. She took part in the evacuation of the British Expeditionary Force from Dunkirk in May 1940 and was also at the Normandy landings in June 1944. After the war she was returned to her owners, in 1945.

RMS STRATHAIRD Built by Vickers Armstrong, Barrow, and launched 18 July 1931 for the Peninsular & Oriental Steam Navigation Company. She was requisitioned on 26 August 1939 for service as a troopship, serving as such until released on 20 September 1946 for refit and return to her owners. She continued in service until sold and broken up in Hong Kong in 1961.

RMS STRATHNAVAR Built by Vickers Armstrong, Barrow, and launched on 5 February 1931 for the Peninsular & Oriental Steam Navigation Company, she was requisitioned on 7 January 1940 for service as a troopship. She served until October 1948 when she was released for refit and returned to her owners. She continued in service until broken up in Hong Kong in April 1962.

MV TARAKAN Built by Feyenoord, Rotterdam and launched in 1930 for the Koninklijke Nederlandsche Stoomvaart Maatschappij NV of Amsterdam. From a class of six ships five survived the war to continue trading in the immediate post-war years.

RFA TEAKOL   Built by Short, Sunderland, and launched on 17 August 1917, she did not remain in Admiralty service for long, as immediately after the First World War had ended many naval and auxiliary ships were laid up and paid off. She was sold on 29 January 1920 and renamed *San Dario*.

RFA THERMOL Built by Caledonian Shipbuilding Company, Greenock, and launched on 29 April 1916, she served on many naval stations around the world, survived the war, and was handed to the Ministry of War Transport on 8 November 1946, and later sold.

SS TORDENE Built by Gray, West Hartlepool, and launched in 1936 for the Dene Shipping Company Ltd, she survived the war after many convoy duties. She is pictured here in Falmouth Bay on 13 May 1946 with a slight list to port, but with many of her wartime fittings still in place.

SY TUSCARORA Built in 1897 she was hired by the Admiralty in January 1940 for service on anti-submarine duties, serving until 1946 when she was returned to her owners.

SS TYNWALD Built by Vickers Armstrong, Barrow, and launched on 16 December 1936 for the Isle of Man Steam Packet Company. She was requisitioned in July 1940 and converted to an anti-aircraft ship. She took part in the evacuation of the British Expeditionary Force at Dunkirk in May 1940 and later was among an armada of ships at the landings in North Africa (Operation Torch). On 9 November 1942 *Tynwald* was attacked by German aircraft as she returned to Algiers to pick up another assault force off Bougie. The landings were completed on 11 November and, when the port had been secured, she moved into the harbour on the 12th but set off a mine laid earlier by the Italian submarine *Argo* and sank.

SS UGANDA Built by Barclay Curle & Company, Glasgow, for the British India Line for service on the East Africa route with sister ship *Kenya*. She came under P & O ownership in December 1972. 0n 13 April 1982 she was requisitioned for service as a hospital ship during the Falklands crisis. After return to her owners she was laid up in the River Fal for twelve months, and despite attempts to save her she was sold for breaking up. In April 1986 she left bound for Taiwan to be broken up, but like many veterans of war, the breaker's yard was not for her and she was caught in a typhoon and driven ashore where she turned on her side and was broken up in situ.

SS ULSTER QUEEN Built by Harland & Wolff, Belfast, and launched on 28 March 1929 for the Belfast Steamship Company. In February 1940 she ran aground in Ramsey Bay. After refloating and refitting she was requisitioned by the Admiralty for service as an anti-aircraft ship and was fitted with three twin 4-inch, two quad 2-pounders and four two-quad 0.5-inch AA machine guns. Her outline had changed as she lost her after funnel and both masts, while her poop deck was levelled. On completion she joined the Irish Sea Escort Force but was soon back in the shipyard for repairs to damage received due to a storm. She later went to Iceland to join Convoy PQ15 (Russian convoy). She was later converted to a fighter direction ship, and was returned to her owners after the war to continue trading.

SS ULYSSES Built by Workman Clark, Belfast, in October 1913 for Alfred Holt & Co. (China Mutual Steam Navigation Company Ltd). Her service run was Glasgow, Liverpool to Australia, and she was one of the last ships to sail from Hong Kong before the Japanese occupation. On 11 April 1942 whilst off the coast of America she was torpedoed by the U160 and sunk.

SS VEENDAM Built by Harland & Wolff, Govan, for the Nederlandsch-Amerikaansche Stoomvaart Maatschappij and launched in 1923. On 11 May 1940 she was damaged and caught fire during a German air raid on Rotterdam, and was then taken over by Germany during its occupation of the Netherlands. On 21 June 1941 she became a barracks ship at Gotenhafen, and in March she was at Hamburg. On 4 November 1944 she was bombed by Allied aircraft and in May 1945 was again damaged by Allied aircraft. She was recovered in late May 1945 at Kiel. She underwent repairs and refit in the Netherlands from 1945 to 1947 and was then returned to service with her owners.

MV VENUS Built by Helsingors Jernskibs in 1931 for the Bercenske Dampskibsselskab A/S in 1940, she came under German control in 1941 and became a U-boat target ship until March 1945. On 15 April 1945 she was bombed and sunk at Hamburg. She was raised in 1945 returned to her owners and refitted, re-entering service on 3 May 1948. She is pictured here after the war in Plymouth Sound after running aground.

SS VICEROY OF INDIA Built by Alexander Stephens, Glasgow, on 15 September 1928 for the P & O Steamship Navigation Company. She was requisitioned on 12 November 1940 for service as a troopship. Almost two years to the day later she was torpedoed by the U407 off Oran, Algeria, and taken in tow by HMS *Bodicea*. Attempts to salvage her failed, and she sank.

RFA VISCOL An oiler built by Craig Taylor, Stockton-on-Tees, and launched on 21 February 1916. She survived the Second World War and was sold in 1947 and renamed *Frecciamare*.

SS VOLENDAM Built by Harland & Wolff, Govan, and launched in 1922 as a sister to the *Veendam*. In 1940 she was requisitioned by the British Government and came under Allied control as a troopship, carrying out this work until 1945 when she was returned to her owners. After refit she continued her Atlantic crossings until March 1952 when, as pictured here, she left Rotterdam for the last time bound for the breaker's yard at Hendrik Ido Ambacht near Dordrecht to be broken up.

RFA WAR AFRIDI Built by Duncan, Port Glasgow, and launched on 11 November 1919, she served until 1949. On 1 January of that year she became an oil hulk and continued in that capacity until sold in 1958.

RFA WAR BHARATA Built by Palmers and launched in June 1919, ships of this type were not only used for Admiralty oiler duties but were also used as water carriers, and in times of emergency could be deployed worldwide. She served until 1948 when in March of that year she was placed on the sales list. She arrived at Troon in May 1953 to be broken up.

RFA WAR BRAHMIN Built by Lithgow, Glasgow, and launched on 28 November 1919, she is pictured here in November 1928 arriving at Malta with fresh water from Sicily. As Malta's water supply could not cope with ships calling for water, those passing through Egyptian waters had to call at Malta as a precaution against cholera being carried in the water picked up in Egypt. She served until February 1960 when she arrived at Spezia to be broken up.

RFA WAR DIWAN   Built by Lithgow, Glasgow, and launched on
28 June 1919. On 16 December 1944 whilst in the River Schelde she
struck a mine and was broken in two, both parts sank. Her forepart
was later refloated and taken to Vlissingen.

RFA WAR MEHTAR Built by Armstrong and launched on 9 October 1919, she served the fleet until 19 November 1941, when off Yarmouth she came under attack by German E-boats and was torpedoed by the S104 and sunk.

RFA WAR NAWAB Built by Palmers and launched on 13 June 1919, she served until November 1939 when she became an oil storage hulk at Plymouth. She arrived at Troon in July 1958.

RFA WAR PATHAN Built by Laing, Sunderland, and launched on 19 March 1919, she served on many stations of the RN until 1947 when she was, with her sister *War Nizam*, sold and renamed. The *Nizam* became the *Abzasinghall* and the *Pathan* became the *Basingbank*.

RFA WAR SEPOY Built by W. Gray & Co. Ltd, West Hartlepool, and launched on 5 December 1918. On 19 July 1940 whilst at Dover she was bombed by German aircraft and badly damaged. On 21 July her back broke and she became a constructive total loss. She was sunk as a blockship at the western entrance to Dover harbour on 7 September 1940. The wreck was dispersed in 1964.

RFA WAR SIRDAR Built by Sir James Laing & Sons Ltd, Sunderland, and launched on 6 December 1919. Late in February 1942 she stranded in the Sunda Strait, Java. Later in 1942 she was salved by the Japanese and recommissioned as *Honan Maru*. She was sunk on 28 March 1945 by the USS *Bluegill*.

RFA WAR SUDRA Built by Palmers and launched in May 1919, after many years service she survived the war and was placed on the sales list in 1946. She was sold out commercially and renamed *Germaine*. Many former RFAs were purchased after being paid off as a stop gap whilst shipping companies awaited new constructions to replace ships lost during the war.

MV WARWICK CASTLE   Built by Harland & Wolff, Belfast, and launched in 1930.   She was requisitioned by the Admiralty in September 1939 as a troopship and was then fitted out as an LSI(L)s and was present at the landings in North Africa.   On her way home, west of Portugal, she was torpedoed by U413 and sunk.

SS WASHINGTON Built by the New York Shipbuilding Company, Camden, New Jersey, and launched in 1933. In June 1941 she was requisitioned by the United States Navy for service as a transport and renamed USS *Mount Vernon*. After war service she returned to her owners in January 1946, the two photographs of her show her before the war in her owners' (United States Lines) colours. The second photograph shows her on a call to Plymouth on 10 July 1946, the first time for seven years.

RFA WAVE MONARCH   Built by Harland & Wolff, Govan, and launched on 5 July 1944, she served as a tanker until the mid 1950s when she was reduced to an oil hulk. She was sold in 1950 as the *Noema*.

RMS WINDSOR CASTLE Built by J. Brown & Co., Clydebank, in 1922 for the Union Castle Mail Steamship Company Ltd. She was requisitioned in 1939 for service as a troopship, and on 23 March 1943 whilst bound from the Clyde for Algiers with 2700 troops on board she was attacked west of Algiers by German aircraft, torpedoed and sunk.

MV WORCESTERSHIRE Built by Fairfields and launched in 1931 for Bibby Brothers & Company. She was requisitioned by the Admiralty on 17 September 1939 for service as an armed merchant cruiser. In 1943 she was returned to the Ministry of War Transport for service as a troopship, and she continued trooping duties until October 1947 when she was returned to her owners the same month.